Early TOY Encyclopedias

POKÉMON

by Jill C. Wheeler

Early Encyclopedias

An Imprint of Abdo Reference

abdobooks.com

abdobooks.com

Published by Abdo Reference, a division of ABDO, PO Box 398166, Minneapolis, Minnesota 55439.

Printed in China.
052025
092025

Editor: Christa Kelly
Series Designers: Candice Keimig, Joshua Olson
Production Designer: Ryan Gale

Library of Congress Control Number: 2024949013

Publisher's Cataloging-in-Publication Data

Names: Wheeler, Jill C., author.
Title: Pokémon / by Jill C. Wheeler
Description: Minneapolis, Minnesota: Abdo Reference, 2026 | Series: Early toy encyclopedias | Includes online resources and index.
Identifiers: ISBN 9781098297572 (lib. bdg.) | ISBN 9798384930099 (ebook)
Subjects: LCSH: Pokémon (Game)--Juvenile literature. | Collectible card games--Juvenile literature. | Toys--Juvenile literature. | Television programs--Juvenile literature. | Collectibles--Juvenile literature. | Reference materials--Juvenile literature. | Encyclopedias and dictionaries--Juvenile literature.
Classification: DDC 794.803--dc23

CONTENTS

INTRODUCTION

Pokémon has millions of fans around the world.

Pokémon

Pokémon is an international sensation. The beloved franchise is about a fictional world full of monsters called Pokémon. Each Pokémon looks and acts differently. Each has special skills. In the Pokémon world, humans can catch Pokémon and train them. Trainers face off in Pokémon battles.

Their Pokémon battle to show their power and their trainer's skill.

Satoshi Tajiri

Pokémon began as an idea in the mind of Satoshi Tajiri. Tajiri lived in Japan. He liked video games. Tajiri began publishing a magazine about video games at age 17. The magazine was called *Game Freak*.

Dr. Bug

When Tajiri was young, he liked collecting bugs. His friends called him Dr. Bug. This love for collecting creatures led him to create Pokémon.

Tajiri was born in 1965 in Tokyo, Japan.

Making Games

Tajiri eventually decided that he wanted to make games. He started a video game company also called Game Freak. He designed a few games for a Japanese company called Nintendo.

The Game Freak company was founded on April 26, 1989, in Tokyo, Japan.

More than 118 million Game Boys have been sold around the world.

Game Boy

In 1989, Nintendo released a handheld game system called the Game Boy. The company sold a cable that could link two Game Boys. This gave Tajiri an idea. He imagined a game about collecting creatures called Pocket Monsters. The cable could let users link their Game Boys and trade creatures.

Pokémon Is Born

Tajiri shared his idea with an illustrator friend named Ken Sugimori. They brought the idea to Nintendo. Nintendo was unsure about the idea. But Tajiri convinced Nintendo to make the game.

Sugimori drew much of the original artwork for the Pokémon games.

***Pocket Monsters Red* and *Green* players started with a Bulbasaur, Charmander, or Squirtle Pocket Monster.**

Pocket Monsters Red and *Green*

Tajiri and Sugimori worked with Nintendo for six years to bring their idea to life. They designed a game centered on a boy who wanted to become a great Pocket Monster trainer. The player had to defeat powerful trainers and collect one of every Pocket Monster to complete the game.

Atsuko Nishida

Atsuko Nishida is an artist. She designed many popular Pokémon, including Pikachu, Bulbasaur, Charmander, and Squirtle.

Trading Pocket Monsters

Game Freak made two versions of the game. Some creatures were exclusive to each version. This meant that players had to trade with each other to collect certain monsters. Trading also allowed some monsters to change forms. This is called evolving. Evolving made creatures stronger.

A Massive Success

Pocket Monsters Red and *Green* were released in Japan in 1996. The games were a hit. Players used Game Boy cables to trade and battle with other players. The game sold more than one million copies within a year.

Pokémon Day

The first Pokémon games were released in Japan on February 27. This day is now known as Pokémon Day.

After the success of *Pocket Monsters Red* and *Green*, *Pocket Monsters Blue* was released in Japan in December 1996.

A Global Sensation

The first games were such a success that they were translated into other languages. The translations shortened the franchise's title to *Pokémon*. The games were released in the United States in 1998. They were renamed *Pokémon Red* and *Blue*. The games sold more than 15 million copies worldwide.

Slogans

Pokémon's English slogan is "Gotta Catch 'Em All!" This tagline was made to encourage Pokémon collecting. The Japanese slogan translates to "Get Pokémon!"

The video game reviewers at the entertainment site IGN gave *Pokémon Red* and *Blue* a perfect score.

Decades after its beginnings, Pokémon remains a beloved franchise.

Pokémon Today

Today, Pokémon is the highest-earning media franchise in history. The Pokémon world spans video games, trading cards, anime, manga, toys, and more. It has become one of the most beloved brands in the world.

The Pokémon world has hundreds of trainers such as Bonnie, *left*, and Serena, *right*.

Life in the Pokémon World

In the Pokémon world, Pokémon play a big role in everyday life. Pokémon roam wild in forests and mountains. They are found in oceans and cities. Many people have Pokémon partners. These Pokémon travel and work with their human companions.

Pokémon Powers

Pokémon make great friends. They are loyal and fun. But they also have incredible abilities. These abilities are called moves or attacks. Some Pokémon can breathe fire. Others can create windstorms. Some can even time travel. Each species has different abilities.

FUN FACT!

Some Pokémon have different features depending on their gender.

Pokémon Regions

The Pokémon world has different regions. Some regions have unique Pokémon. The same Pokémon may have slight differences across regions.

Kanto Vulpix and Alolan Vulpix are the same Pokémon but are from different regions.

The first Pokémon that were introduced came from the Kanto region.

Real-World Similarities

Many Pokémon regions are based on places in the real world. Kanto and Johto are based on places in Japan. So are Hoenn and Sinnoh. Unova and Alola are based on places in the United States. Galar is inspired by the United Kingdom. Kalos is inspired by France. Paldea is based on Spain and Portugal.

In Japanese, Poké Balls are known as "Monster Balls."

Poké Balls

People can catch a Pokémon by throwing a Poké Ball. Poké Balls are hollow balls that can comfortably store Pokémon. A Pokémon shrinks down to fit inside. Tossing the ball again lets the Pokémon out.

Catching Pokémon

Weak or friendly Pokémon can be caught just by throwing a Poké Ball. But stronger Pokémon are harder to catch. Most Pokémon have to be battled before being caught.

Types of Poké Balls

There are more than 25 different types of Poké Balls. Each has different abilities. Fast Balls catch speedy Pokémon. Heal Balls heal Pokémon as they're caught.

Trainers use their Pokémon to battle the new monster. The trainer can catch the Pokémon once it is worn down.

Pokémon video games allow players to fight in Pokémon battles.

Training Pokémon

People must train their Pokémon by using them in battles. Training teaches Pokémon new skills. It helps Pokémon grow stronger. Trainers must learn to work with their Pokémon. They may also teach their Pokémon to work together.

Trainers often have multiple Pokémon. Some Pokémon get along with each other. Others do not.

Charmander evolves into Charmeleon. Charmeleon evolves into Charizard.

Evolving Pokémon

Pokémon can evolve when they get stronger. This means that they change into new Pokémon. The new Pokémon is a stronger version of its original form. Some types of Pokémon can evolve twice. Others can evolve once. Some have only one form. They do not evolve.

Many Pokémon nurses work with Pokémon called Chansey. Chansey are good healers.

Jobs in Pokémon

Many people in the Pokémon world have jobs that also exist in the real world. But others have jobs related to Pokémon. Some people work as Pokémon nurses. These people help sick and injured Pokémon. Some people study Pokémon. Others work as Pokémon breeders. Still others make Poké Balls.

Pokémon Trainers

Many people work as Pokémon trainers. These people devote their time to finding Pokémon. Then they train them. They might battle their Pokémon against the Pokémon of other trainers. Some travel to different regions to find rare Pokémon.

People can usually apply to become Pokémon trainers at age 10.

Pokédex Numbering

Each Pokémon has an official number in the Pokédex. Bulbasaur is #0001. Its evolution, Ivysaur, is #0002. Pikachu is #0025.

Pokédex

Pokémon trainers often work to complete their Pokédex. The Pokédex is a digital device that lists each discovered and caught Pokémon. It describes each Pokémon and lists its average height and weight. Filling the Pokédex takes a long time. There are more than 1,000 discovered Pokémon.

Pokémon fans can buy a toy Pokédex.

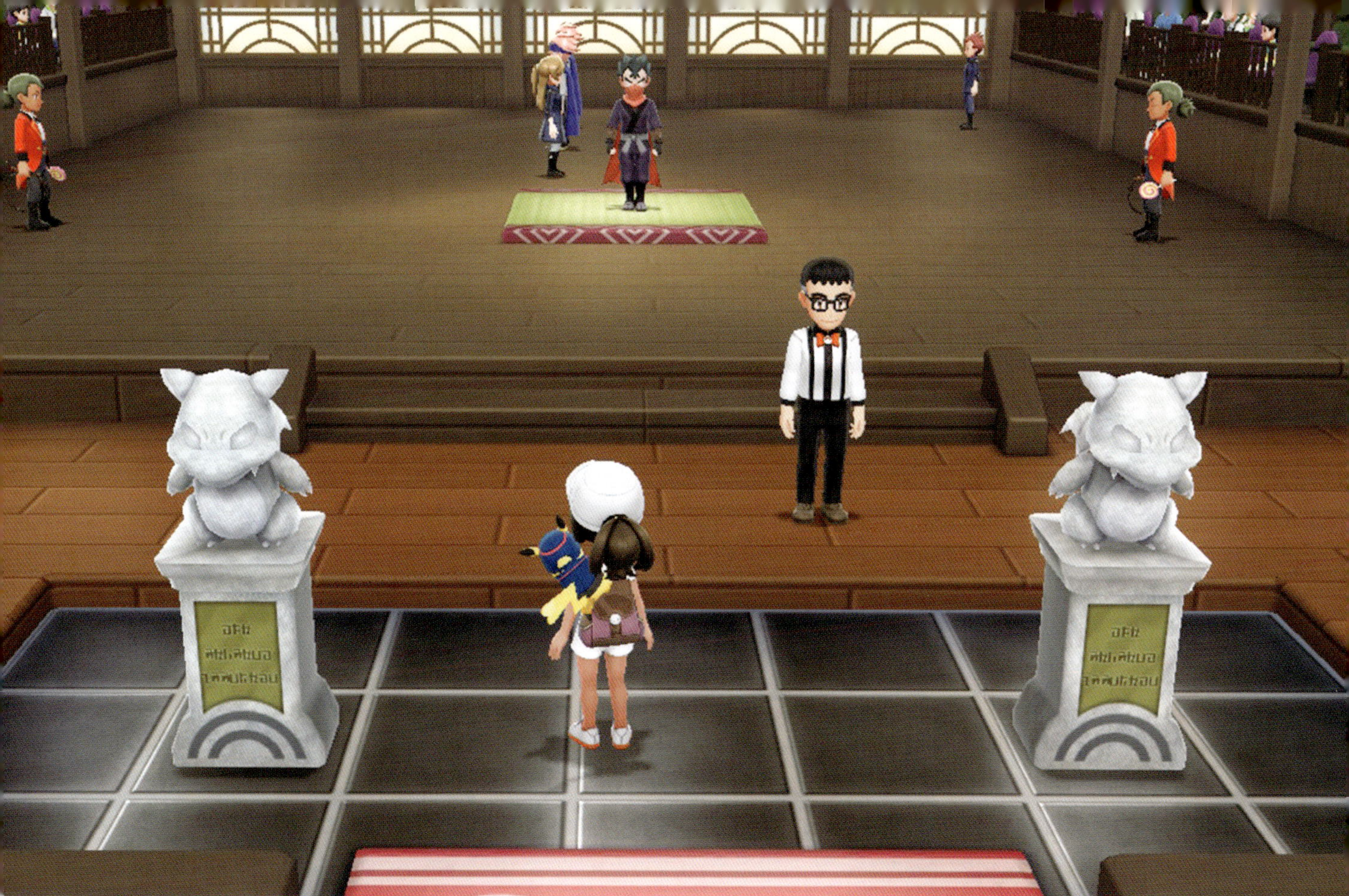

Many Gyms have themes. The Gym Leaders at these Gyms use only one type of Pokémon.

Gyms

Trainers often train their Pokémon at Gyms. These are places where trainers gather to battle. The best trainers become Gym Leaders. Trainers can test their strength by challenging Gym Leaders. Those who beat a Gym Leader earn an item called a Gym Badge.

In many games, players need to defeat a group of powerful trainers called the Elite Four to become the champion of the Pokémon League.

Pokémon League

Trainers who want to compete can join the Pokémon League. The Pokémon League organizes competitions. Pokémon trainers from different areas come together and compete in Pokémon battles to prove they are the best of the trainers.

Villains

Some people view Pokémon as tools instead of partners. They use their Pokémon to steal from others. Some even want to take over the world. These people are villains in the Pokémon world.

Both people and Pokémon can be villains.

Team Rocket

Team Rocket is a group of criminals who steal Pokémon. They are among the most well-known villains in the Pokémon world. Pokémon trainers battle them to protect innocent Pokémon and people.

Jessie, James, and Meowth are the most famous members of Team Rocket.

Articuno, Zapdos, and Moltres were the first Legendary Pokémon ever released.

Legendary and Mythical Pokémon

Pokémon villains often want to catch Legendary and Mythical Pokémon. These Pokémon are rare and powerful. Some are treated like gods. These Pokémon are often found only in a specific region. Mythical Pokémon are the rarest. Just over 20 species have been discovered.

FUN FACT!

Some Pokémon change types when they evolve.

Pokémon Types

Pokémon are grouped into types. Pokémon of the same type share similar battle skills. They can perform similar moves. They also have similar strengths and weaknesses. The first Pokémon games had 15 types. Later games added four new types.

Single and Dual

Some Pokémon have a single type. Others have two types. Monsters with two types are called dual-type Pokémon. They carry both the advantages and disadvantages of each of their types.

Jigglypuff is a dual-type Pokémon. It is Normal type and Fairy type.

Pokémon Types

Each Pokémon species is assigned one or two of the below types.
No Pokémon begin with a nineteenth type, Stellar type.

Water type

GROUND

Ground type

POISON

Poison type

Fire type

Rock type

Bug type

Grass type

Ice type

Fighting type

Normal type

Psychic type

Flying type

Electric type

Ghost type

Dragon type

Dark type

STEEL

Steel type

Fairy type

Moves

Like Pokémon, moves are sorted into different types. Each move can have only a single type. The move's type reflects what the move does. For example, the move Water Gun squirts water. It is a Water-type attack. Moves that match the attacking Pokémon's type do more damage to opponents.

Trainers help their Pokémon learn new moves.

Water Type

The most common Pokémon type is Water. Many Water-type Pokémon live in water. Water-type Pokémon are resistant to Fire, Ice, and Steel-type moves. They are weak against Electric and Grass-type moves. Water-type moves are strong against Fire, Ground, and Rock-type Pokémon. These moves are not very strong against Water, Grass, and Dragon-type Pokémon.

The Fire-type Pokémon Monferno uses its flaming tail as a weapon.

Fire Type

Fire-type Pokémon were rare in early games. Fire-type Pokémon are resistant to Fire, Ice, Bug, Steel, and Fairy-type moves. They are weak against Water, Ground, and Rock-type moves. Fire-type moves are strong against Grass, Ice, Bug, and Steel-type Pokémon. These moves are not very strong against Fire, Water, Rock, and Dragon-type Pokémon.

Grass Type

Many Grass-type Pokémon resemble plants. Grass-type Pokémon are resistant to Water, Grass, Electric, and Ground-type moves. They are weak against Fire, Ice, Poison, Flying, and Bug-type moves. Grass-type moves are strong against Water, Ground, and Rock-type Pokémon. These moves are not very effective against Fire, Grass, Poison, Flying, Bug, Dragon, and Steel-type Pokémon.

Sprigatito is a Grass-type Pokémon. Its fur absorbs sunlight and turns it into energy.

Ditto is a Normal-type Pokémon. It can shape-shift into any other Pokémon.

Normal Type

There are more than 130 Normal-type Pokémon. This makes it one of the most common types. Normal-type Pokémon are not resistant to any moves. However, they are immune to Ghost-type moves. They are weak against Fighting-type moves. Normal-type moves are not strong against any Pokémon. They are weak against Rock and Steel-type Pokémon. The moves do no damage to Ghost-type Pokémon.

Electric Type

Electric-type Pokémon can control, store, or make electricity. They are resistant to Electric, Steel, and Flying-type moves. They are weak against Ground-type moves. Electric-type moves are strong against Water and Flying-type Pokémon. These moves are not very effective against Grass, Electric, or Dragon-type Pokémon. Electric-type moves do no damage to Ground-type Pokémon.

Raichu is an Electric-type Pokémon. It evolves from Pikachu.

Ground Type

Ground-type Pokémon can be found in caves and rocky areas. They are resistant to Poison and Rock-type moves. They are immune to Electric-type moves. Ground-type Pokémon are weak against Water, Grass, and Ice-type moves. Ground-type moves are strong against Fire, Electric, Poison, Rock, and Steel-type Pokémon. These moves are not very effective against Grass or Bug-type Pokémon. Ground-type moves do no damage to Flying-type Pokémon.

Sandslash is a Ground-type Pokémon. It protects itself by rolling up into a spiky ball.

The Rock-type Pokémon Cranidos can be resurrected from fossils.

Rock Type

Many Rock-type Pokémon are covered in a protective rock coating. Rock-type Pokémon are resistant to Normal, Fire, Poison, and Flying-type moves. They are weak against Water, Grass, Fighting, Ground, and Steel-type moves. Rock-type moves are strong against Fire, Ice, Flying, and Bug-type Pokémon. These moves are not very effective against Fighting, Ground, or Steel-type Pokémon.

Galarian Darumaka is an Ice-type Pokémon. It uses its freezing breath to make snowballs.

Ice Type

Ice-type Pokémon generally live in cold areas. They are resistant to Ice-type moves. They are weak against Fire, Fighting, Rock, and Steel-type moves. Ice-type moves are strong against Grass, Ground, Flying, and Dragon-type Pokémon. These moves are not very effective against Fire, Water, Ice, or Steel-type Pokémon.

Psychic Type

Psychic-type Pokémon are normally very smart. They are resistant to Fighting and Psychic-type moves. They are weak against Bug, Ghost, and Dark-type moves. Psychic-type moves are strong against Fighting and Poison-type Pokémon. These moves are not very effective against Psychic or Steel-type Pokémon. Psychic-type moves do no damage to Dark-type Pokémon.

The Psychic-type Pokémon Drowzee eats people's dreams.

Greavard is a Ghost-type Pokémon. It loves people but slowly drains their life force.

Ghost Type

Ghost-type Pokémon often live in graveyards and abandoned buildings. They are resistant to Poison and Bug-type moves. They are immune to Normal and Fighting-type moves. Ghost-type Pokémon are weak against Ghost and Dark-type moves. Ghost-type moves are strong against Psychic and Ghost-type Pokémon. These moves are not very effective against Dark-type Pokémon. Ghost-type moves do no damage to Normal-type Pokémon.

Poison Type

Poison-type Pokémon are often based on toxic plants or animals. They are resistant to Grass, Fighting, Poison, Bug, and Fairy-type moves. They are weak against Ground and Psychic-type moves. Poison-type moves are strong against Grass and Fairy-type Pokémon. These moves are not very effective against Poison, Ground, Rock, or Ghost-type Pokémon. Poison-type moves do no damage to Steel-type Pokémon.

Bug Type

Many Bug-type Pokémon live in forests. They are resistant to Grass, Fighting, and Ground-type moves. They are weak against Fire, Flying, and Rock-type moves. Bug-type moves are strong against Grass, Psychic, and Dark-type Pokémon. These moves are not very effective against Fire, Fighting, Poison, Flying, Ghost, Steel, and Fairy-type Pokémon.

Caterpie is a Bug-type Pokémon. It has suction cups on its feet to help it climb trees.

Fighting Type

Fighting-type Pokémon are built to battle. They are resistant to Bug, Rock, and Dark-type moves. They are weak against Flying, Psychic, and Fairy-type moves. Fighting-type moves are strong against Normal, Ice, Rock, Dark, and Steel-type Pokémon. These moves are not very effective against Poison, Flying, Psychic, Bug, and Fairy-type Pokémon. Fighting-type moves do no damage to Ghost-type Pokémon.

Corvisquire is a Flying-type Pokémon. It is smart enough to use tools in battles.

Flying Type

Flying-type Pokémon are almost always dual type. They are resistant to Grass and Bug-type moves. They are immune to Ground-type moves. These Pokémon are weak against Electric, Ice, and Rock-type moves. Flying-type moves are strong against Grass, Fighting, and Bug-type Pokémon. These moves are not very effective against Electric, Rock, or Steel-type Pokémon.

Dragon Type

Dragon-type Pokémon are among the strongest monsters. They are resistant to Fire, Water, Grass, and Electric-type moves. They are weak against Ice, Dragon, and Fairy-type moves. Dragon-type moves are strong against Dragon-type Pokémon. These moves are not very effective against Steel-type Pokémon. Dragon-type moves do no damage to Fairy-type Pokémon.

Dratini is a Dragon-type Pokémon. It's so rare that people used to think it was a myth.

Dark Type

Dark-type Pokémon were introduced in the games *Pokémon Gold* and *Silver.* Dark-type Pokémon are resistant to Ghost and Dark-type moves. They are immune to Psychic-type moves. Dark-type Pokémon are weak against Fighting, Bug, and Fairy-type moves. Dark-type moves are strong against Psychic and Ghost-type Pokémon. These moves are not very effective against Fighting, Dark, or Fairy-type Pokémon.

The Dark-type Pokémon Poochyena uses its strong sense of smell to track prey.

Steel Type

Steel-type Pokémon first appeared in *Pokémon Gold* and *Silver*. Steel-type Pokémon are resistant to Normal, Grass, Ice, Flying, Psychic, Bug, Rock, Dragon, Steel, and Fairy-type moves. They are immune to Poison-type moves. Steel-type Pokémon are weak against Fire, Fighting, and Ground-type moves. Steel-type moves are strong against Ice, Rock, and Fairy-type Pokémon. These moves are not very effective against Fire, Water, Electric, or Steel-type Pokémon.

The Fairy-type Pokémon Togepi is a symbol of good luck.

Fairy Type

The games *Pokémon X* and *Y* introduced Fairy-type Pokémon. Fairy-type Pokémon are resistant to Fighting, Bug, and Dark-type moves. They are immune to Dragon-type moves. Fairy-type Pokémon are weak against Poison and Steel-type moves. Fairy-type moves are strong against Fighting, Dragon, and Dark-type Pokémon. These moves are not very effective against Fire, Poison, or Steel-type Pokémon.

Stellar Type

Stellar-type Pokémon were introduced in *Pokémon Scarlet* and *Violet*. Unlike other types, no Pokémon or moves naturally have the Stellar type. Instead, Pokémon temporarily become Stellar type in a process called Terastallization. This process makes Pokémon look crystallized. Stellar-type moves are strong against other Terastallized Pokémon.

Some rare Pokémon cards feature Terastallized Pokémon.

Pokémon Trading Card Game

Game Freak launched the Pokémon Trading Card Game (TCG) in 1996. The game is played with two players. Each player starts with a deck made up of Pokémon, Energy, and Trainer cards. The players take turns battling against each other's Pokémon.

FUN FACT!

More than 53 billion Pokémon TCG cards have been produced.

The Pokémon Trading Card Game is popular with people of all ages.

Some players have multiple decks of cards.

Deck Building

Players start with a 60-card deck. They build these decks before playing the game. Players must carefully consider which cards will work well together.

Pokémon Cards

Each Pokémon card has art of a Pokémon. The Pokémon's name is written at the top of the card. Each card includes a fun fact about the featured Pokémon.

Attacks and Abilities

The center of the card details the Pokémon's attacks and abilities. Attacks do damage to the opponent's Pokémon. Abilities provide special effects. For example, some allow players to draw extra cards. Different Pokémon have different attacks and abilities.

Special Conditions

Some attacks give the opponent's Pokémon special conditions. These conditions include Asleep, Burned, Confused, Paralyzed, and Poisoned. Evolving the Pokémon or retreating removes these conditions.

Pokémon Cards

Most Pokémon cards include similar information.

Eevee is a Normal-type Pokémon in the video games but a Colorless type in the TCG.

Pokémon TCG Types

In the top-right corner of each Pokémon card is a symbol that represents the Pokémon's type. These types are sometimes different from the types in the video games. Most Pokémon have only one type per card.

Type Changes

The card game has only ten types. These types are Grass, Fire, Water, Lightning, Fighting, Psychic, Colorless, Darkness, Metal, and Dragon. Some of the original types were renamed for the card game. Other types were combined into another category.

The Pokémon TCG used to have a Fairy type. Today, Fairy-type Pokémon are grouped with Psychic-type Pokémon.

Hit Points

To the left of the type symbol is a number. This number is the Pokémon's Hit Points. This is how much attack damage the creature can take before being knocked out.

Each Pokémon has between 30 and 350 Hit Points.

Evolving Pokémon

Players can evolve their Pokémon. Each player starts out by playing a Basic Pokémon. This is an unevolved Pokémon.

Players can place a Pokémon card with the evolved form of a Basic Pokémon on top of the original card. The evolved Pokémon has new attacks and is often stronger.

Squirtle evolves into Wartortle. Wartortle evolves into Blastoise.

Trainer Cards

Trainer cards have a variety of effects. There are four types. Item cards allow players to draw more cards. Tool cards can restore health or boost a Pokémon's strength. Supporter cards include trainers who offer abilities such as allowing players to draw more cards. Stadium cards change the battle location. This causes effects such as boosting attacks for Pokémon of specific types.

Supporter cards are based on characters from the Pokémon world.

Energy Cards

Energy cards attach to Pokémon cards. These cards are used to power attacks. More powerful attacks require more energy. Different attacks may also require different types of energy. There are Fire, Water, Grass, Darkness, Fairy, Lightning, Fighting, Psychic, and Metal-type Energy cards.

Most decks should have between 8 and 12 Energy cards.

Winning the Game

Before the game begins, players place six cards from their decks to the side. These are the players' prize cards. Knocking out an opponent's Pokémon earns a player a prize card.

Pokémon TCG tournaments are held around the world.

The first player to collect all six prize cards wins. Players can also win by knocking out all the opponent's active Pokémon.

Moving to North America

Pokémon TCG was a major success in Japan. Many fans enjoyed playing the game. Others loved collecting the cards. The game debuted in North America in 1999. Its popularity grew.

Some TCG tournaments offer Pokémon cards as prizes for the winners.

The backs of English Pokémon cards generally have the same design.

The Game Grows

As Pokémon TCG became more popular, more cards were released. Some Pokémon appear on hundreds of different cards. More than 18,000 unique cards have been released.

Full Art Cards

A Full Art card has an image that extends along the entire card. These cards are often rarer than normal cards.

International Sensation

Today, Pokémon cards are popular among both collectors and TCG players. The cards have been translated into 14 languages. They're sold in 89 countries and regions. Many cities have Pokémon Leagues where people can gather and play the card game. Some cities have conventions where people display their card collections.

Pokémon cards are printed in many languages, including Japanese, English, French, Italian, German, and Spanish.

Pokémon Art

Some people collect Pokémon cards for their unique art. The images on the cards have many different art styles. Some are paintings. Others are photos taken of clay sculptures. Still others are photos of crocheted Pokémon plushies.

Asako Ito crochets Pokémon to include on cards.

Ken Sugimori designed art for some of the cards in the Pokémon base set.

Illustrators

About 200 people have provided art for Pokémon cards. These people are called illustrators. Most cards list the cards' illustrators. One of the first Pokémon card illustrators was Ken Sugimori. He has designed art for more than 900 cards.

In 2024, more than 10,000 entries were submitted to the Pokémon Illustration Contest.

Illustration Contest

Fans can illustrate cards too. The Pokémon Company occasionally holds illustration contests. People from around the world design cards. They submit their art to the contest. Several winners are chosen. The winners receive a cash prize. Some of the winners have their illustrations placed on cards.

Rare Cards

Some cards are rarer than others. Collectors can look for a rarity symbol on the bottom of a card to determine how rare the card is. Cards with a circle are common. Cards with a diamond are uncommon. Cards with a star are rare.

Rare cards usually feature Pokémon with stronger abilities.

Holographic Cards

Some cards have a shiny finish over the pictures. These cards are called holographics. Cards with a shiny background are called reverse holographics. Holographics and reverse holographics are more sought after than regular cards.

Holographic cards are also known as holos or foils.

Buying Cards

More cards are added as more monsters join the Pokémon world. Cards are added in sets. A single expansion set can have more than 200 new cards.

Players can buy new cards in bulk in Elite Trainer Boxes. The cards in the boxes are random. This means that buyers do not know what they are getting. Players looking for smaller amounts of new cards can buy booster packs. These packs come with ten random cards.

More than 100 Pokémon TCG expansion sets have been released.

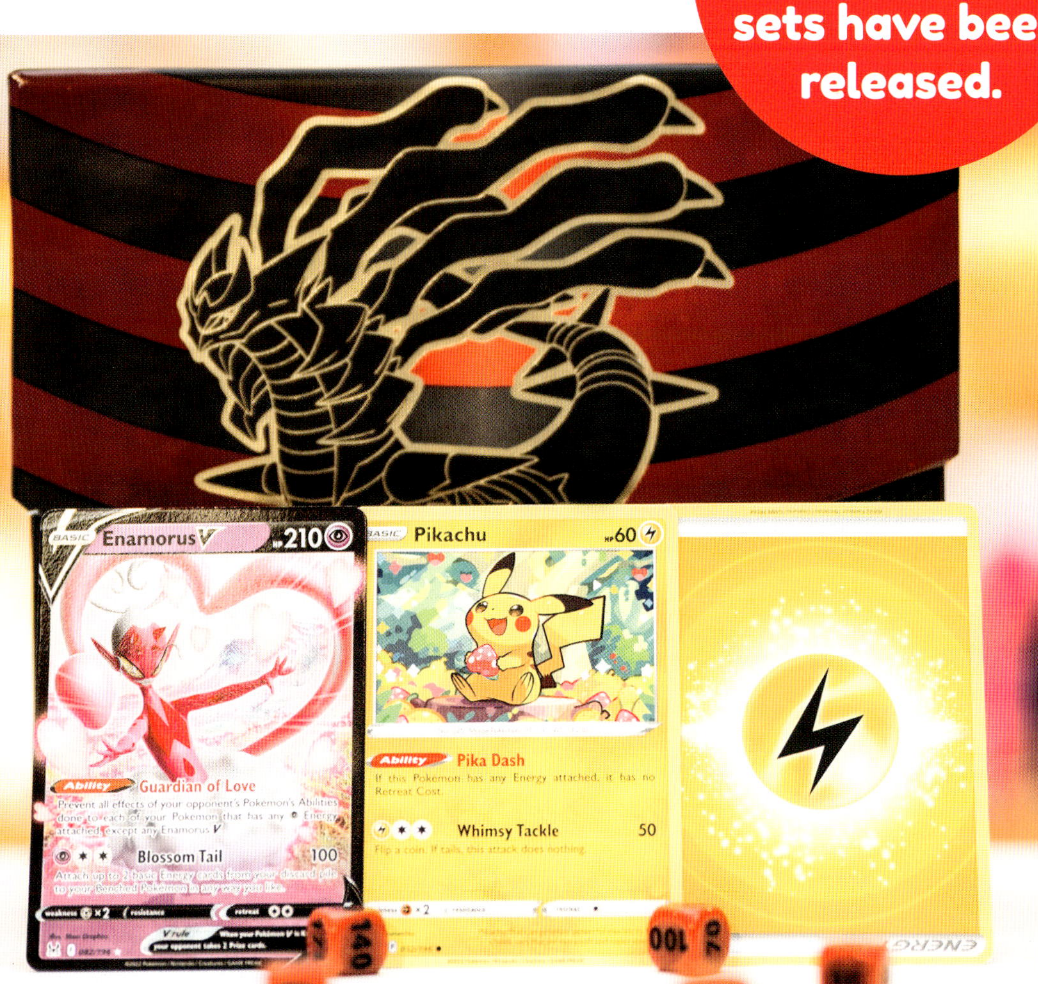

People can buy cards from local gaming stores and from online businesses.

Singles

Some gaming stores sell singles. These are individual cards. This allows buyers to choose their cards. Some common cards cost only a few cents. Rare cards cost thousands of dollars.

Illustrator Pikachu

Winners of a 1998 drawing contest in Japan received Pikachu Illustrator cards. Only a few were made. One sold for more than $5 million in 2021.

Cards in good condition cost more than cards in poor condition. Professional graders determine the condition of rare cards.

Playing Online

Pokémon TCG Online was released in 2011. The game allowed people to play Pokémon TCG on the internet. People could compete against computers or against real people. In 2023, the game was replaced by the updated *Pokémon TCG Live*.

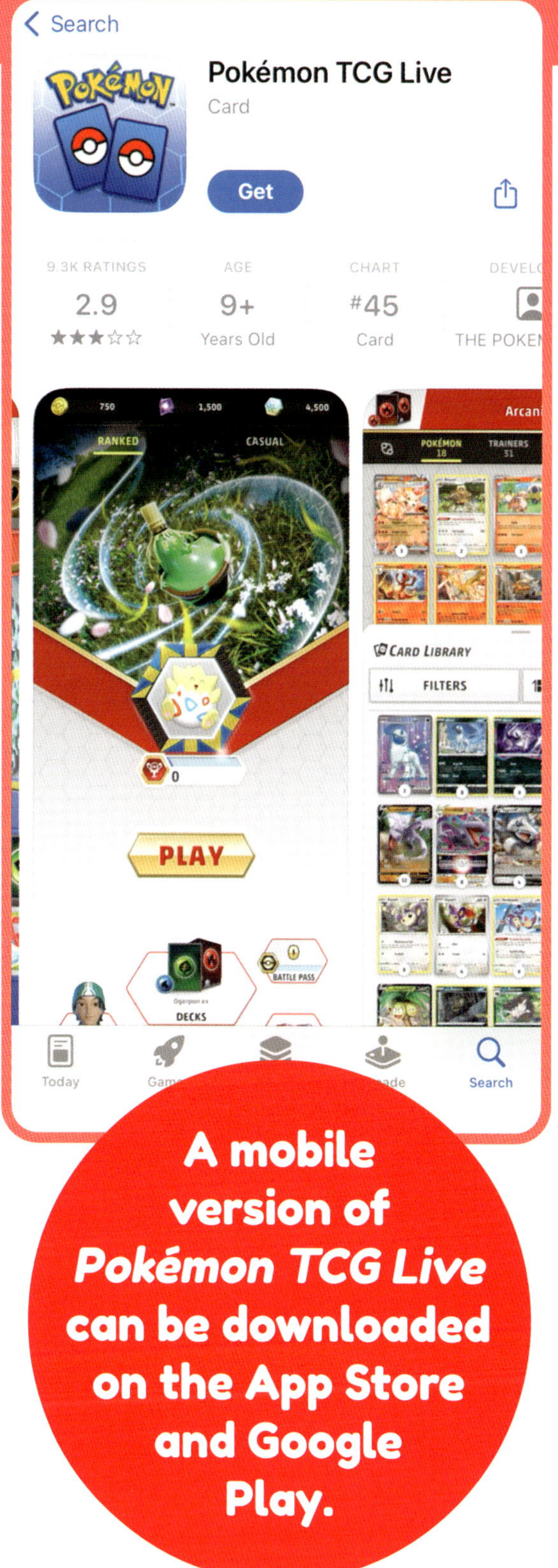

A mobile version of *Pokémon TCG Live* can be downloaded on the App Store and Google Play.

FUN FACT!

In the Japanese version of the anime, Ash is named Satoshi after the creator of Pokémon.

Pokémon Anime

With the Pokémon video games and card game making waves across Japan, the franchise was turned into an anime. It was called *Pokémon: The Series*. The first episode aired in 1997. The show follows a young boy named Ash Ketchum on his journey to become a Pokémon Master.

Ash's first Pokémon was a Pikachu.

Ash and Pikachu

In the first episode, Ash chooses a Pikachu to be his Pokémon partner. Pikachu is an Electric-type Pokémon. Ash and Pikachu quickly become best friends. They travel across the Pokémon world. The two meet new Pokémon and battle in the Pokémon League.

FUN FACT!

Ash's Pikachu eats berries and apples, but its favorite food is ketchup.

When the Pokémon anime was released, it was targeted toward children. But the show attracted people of all ages.

The Anime Goes International

The show was a hit in Japan. It was soon translated for English audiences. The series aired in the United States in 1998. Audiences loved it. The series lasted for 25 seasons. It finished with more than 1,000 episodes.

Pokémon Movies

Ash's adventures continued in the Pokémon movies. *Pokémon: The First Movie* was released in 1998. More than 20 Pokémon movies have been released since. The movies generally focus on Legendary and Mythical Pokémon.

Manga

Japanese comic books are called manga. Several Pokémon manga series have been released. The manga has sold more than 150 million copies.

The Pokémon movies have earned more than $1 billion worldwide.

Detective Pikachu

A live-action Pokémon movie was released in 2019. It was called *Detective Pikachu*. The movie follows a young man named Tim as he and a talking Pikachu look for Tim's father.

Ryan Reynolds voiced Pikachu in *Detective Pikachu*.

Pokémon Horizons

The original Pokémon anime series ended in 2023. A new series called *Pokémon Horizons* began in 2024. The show features a girl named Liko and her Pokémon Sprigatito. Liko and her friends battle against an evil group called the Explorers.

FUN FACT!

One of the characters in *Pokémon Horizons* is a Pikachu who's the captain of an airship.

Many Pokémon from older generations can be caught in new games.

Pokémon Generations

After the success of *Pokémon Red* and *Blue*, Game Freak began working on new games. The first games became known as Generation 1. Each pair of new mainline games was considered a new generation. New generations introduced new Pokémon.

Pokémon Yellow

In 1998, *Pokémon Yellow* was released. The game was a remake of *Pokémon Red* and *Blue*. Most of the features stayed the same. However, the player's starter Pokémon was changed to a Pikachu. This change was made due to the success of the Pokémon anime. Several other characters were also changed to characters from the anime.

Pokémon Yellow was released for the Game Boy.

Pokémon Snap

Pokémon Snap was released in 1999. This game is a spin-off rather than a mainline game. The game focuses on a character named Todd Snap, a Pokémon photographer. Players must explore an island and take pictures of wild Pokémon in their natural habitats.

***Pokémon Snap* was released for the Nintendo 64.**

Pokémon *Gold* and *Silver* sold more than 23 million copies.

Pokémon Gold and *Silver*

Generation 2 of Pokémon was introduced in 1999 with *Pokémon Gold* and *Silver*. The games are for the Game Boy Color. This generation adds 100 new Pokémon. It also introduces Steel and Dark-type Pokémon. The games take place in a new area called the Johto region.

Starter Pokémon

Each mainline game begins with players choosing one of three Pokémon. Players can usually choose a Fire, Water, or Grass-type Pokémon. These Pokémon are called starter Pokémon.

***Pokémon Ruby* and *Sapphire* introduce Mudkip, Torchic, and Treecko as starter Pokémon.**

Pokémon Ruby and *Sapphire*

The third generation of Pokémon games was released in 2002 for the Game Boy Advance. The games are called *Pokémon Ruby* and *Sapphire* and are set in the Hoenn region. *Ruby* and *Sapphire* introduce 135 new monsters.

Pokémon Colosseum

Pokémon Colosseum was released in 2003 for the Nintendo GameCube. It is a spin-off game. Players control a character who had formerly been a villain. The game introduces Shadow Pokémon. These are Pokémon who have been turned evil.

Pokémon Colosseum sold 2.4 million copies worldwide.

Pokémon Mystery Dungeon

Pokémon Mystery Dungeon: Blue Rescue Team and *Red Rescue Team* were released in 2005. These games are spin-offs. Players take on the role of a human who has been turned into a Pokémon. Several other *Pokémon Mystery Dungeon* games have been released since.

Players are given a quiz at the start of *Pokémon Mystery Dungeon*. Their answers determine which Pokémon they become.

Pokémon Ranger players work with Plusle, *left*, or Minun, *right*.

Pokémon Ranger

Pokémon Ranger was released in early 2006 for the Nintendo DS. This game is a spin-off. Players control a Pokémon Ranger. The player uses the DS touch screen to capture Pokémon. The player then uses the Pokémon's attacks to complete missions.

***Pokémon Diamond* and *Pearl* introduce the Legendary Pokémon Palkia, *left*, and Dialga, *right*.**

Pokémon Diamond and Pearl

Pokémon Diamond and *Pearl* ushered in Generation 4 in 2006. The games were made for the Nintendo DS. *Diamond* and *Pearl* introduce 107 new Pokémon. The games take place in the Sinnoh region.

Pokémon Rumble

Pokémon Rumble is a spin-off game released in 2009. It was designed for the Wii. Players must battle against windup toy Pokémon that have come to life. They befriend some of the Pokémon to help them win battles.

***Pokémon Rumble* players begin the game controlling a Rattata.**

Pokémon Black and *White*

Generation 5 began with *Pokémon Black* and *White*. The games were released in 2010 for the Nintendo DS. They introduce a record 156 new Pokémon. These games take place in the Unova region.

FUN FACT!

Japanese gaming magazine *Famitsu* gave *Pokémon Black* and *White* a perfect rating.

Pikachu, *center*, is a Generation 1 Pokémon. Pignite, Dewott, Oshawott, and Snivy, *left to right*, were introduced in Generation 5.

Though unavailable in the original *Pokémon Black* and *White*, Regice can be caught in the sequels.

Pokémon Black 2 and *White 2*

Pokémon Black 2 and *White 2* were released in 2012. The games take place two years after the events in the original *Black* and *White*. The games introduce new areas.

Fennekin was introduced in Generation 6.

Pokémon X and Y

Pokémon X and *Y* were released in 2013. This signaled the start of Generation 6. The games were made for the Nintendo 3DS. *X* and *Y* introduce 72 new Pokémon. They also introduce the Fairy type. The games take place in the Kalos region.

Pokémon Go

Pokémon Go is a smartphone game released in 2016. The game allows users to find Pokémon around their neighborhoods. Players can walk around their towns and catch Pokémon. They can battle friends and help other players catch powerful Pokémon. The game was an international hit.

FUN FACT!

***Pokémon Go* has been downloaded more than one billion times.**

***Pokémon Go* uses special technology to make it look like players are catching Pokémon in the real world.**

***Pokémon Sun* and *Moon* players start by choosing a Rowlet, Litten, or Popplio.**

Pokémon Sun and Moon

Generation 7 began with the 2016 games *Pokémon Sun* and *Moon*. The games were released for the Nintendo 3DS. *Sun* and *Moon* are set in the tropical Alola region. The games introduce 81 new Pokémon. Other Pokémon get new Alolan forms. The games also add a new game mechanic called Z-Moves. These moves add extra power to certain battle moves.

Pokémon Ultra Sun and *Ultra Moon*

Pokémon Ultra Sun and *Ultra Moon* were released in 2017 for the Nintendo 3DS. These games include new content that isn't in the regular *Sun* and *Moon* games. In addition to storyline changes, the games add five new Pokémon.

The Mythical Pokémon Zeroara was introduced in *Ultra Sun* and *Ultra Moon*.

Pokémon Sword and Shield

Generation 8 launched in 2019 with the release of *Pokémon Sword* and *Shield*. The games were created for the Nintendo Switch. *Sword* and *Shield* take place in the Galar region. The games add 81 new Pokémon. Other familiar Pokémon are given new Galarian forms.

***Pokémon Sword* and *Shield* introduce giant monsters called Dynamax Pokémon.**

Pokémon Legends: Arceus **is the first title in the** ***Pokémon Legends*** **game series.**

Pokémon Legends: Arceus

Pokémon Legends: Arceus is a spin-off game. It was released in 2022 for the Nintendo Switch. The game follows a Pokémon trainer who was sent back in time. Players must travel across the open-world map to complete their Pokédex.

***Pokémon Scarlet* and *Violet* introduced Legendary Pokémon Koraidon, *left*, and Miraidon, *right*.**

Pokémon Scarlet and *Violet*

The 2022 games *Pokémon Scarlet* and *Violet* ushered in Generation 9. The games were made for the Nintendo Switch. *Scarlet* and *Violet* take place in the Paldea region. They introduce 105 new Pokémon as well as Paradox Pokémon. These are prehistoric and futuristic versions of familiar Pokémon.

Extra Content

In 2023, extra content was released for *Pokémon Scarlet* and *Violet*. The content added new stories. The update came in two parts. The first was called *The Teal Mask*. The second was titled *The Indigo Disk*. The new content allows players to get previously unavailable Pokémon from earlier generations.

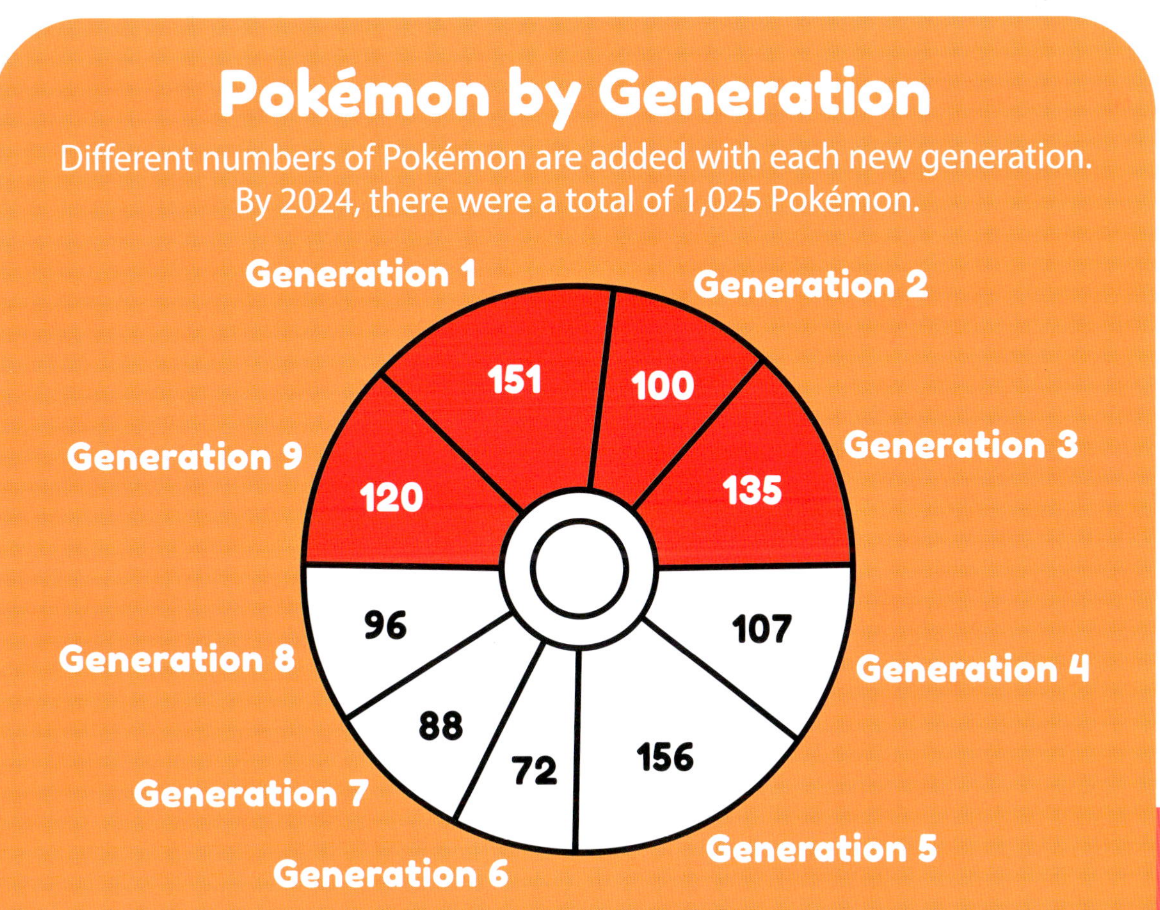

Pokémon Center

The Pokémon Center is an online store that releases official Pokémon merchandise. The store sells a variety of products to allow fans to show their love for Pokémon. In addition to the online store, several countries have physical Pokémon Center stores.

FUN FACT!

People have bought more than $88 billion of Pokémon items.

The Pokémon Center sells merchandise based on hundreds of different Pokémon.

Some figures cost less than ten dollars. Others cost hundreds of dollars.

Action Figures

Action figures let fans of all ages interact with Pokémon. Some action figures are for display. Others feature moving parts for play. Pokémon fans can buy single action figures or purchase figures in sets. The Jazwares company is known for its highly detailed action figures.

People can sometimes buy opened blind box figures online.

Blind Box Figures

Some Pokémon figures come in sealed boxes. Buyers don't know which figure they will get until they open the boxes. These are called blind boxes. People may have to buy several to get the figure they want.

Blind Box Sets

Some blind boxes contain part of a bigger set. Each box contains a Pokémon and a few accessories. People have to buy several boxes to complete the set. Re-Ment is one company that sells Pokémon blind box sets.

The Forest Playground is one of Re-Ment's Pokémon blind box sets.

Funko Pop! Figures

Toy company Funko added Pokémon to its Pop! line of figures in 2018. The company sells more than 40 Pokémon figures. The figures range from 4 to 18 inches (10 to 46 cm) tall. Collectors can buy individual figures or box sets.

There are several different Funko Pop! versions of Pikachu.

The Nendoroid Pokémon line includes a figure of Red, *left*, a trainer from the Pokémon video games.

Nendoroids

Good Smile Company makes posable action figures called Nendoroids. The company collaborated with Pokémon to make a line of Pokémon Nendoroids. More than ten Pokémon figures are available. The Nendoroids include both Pokémon and trainers.

Gachapon machines release a random capsule, so buyers do not know which gachapon toy they will get.

Gachapon Toys

Gachapon toys fit into small plastic capsules. The capsules are sold through coin-operated vending machines. People can also buy them online. Toy maker Tomy makes many Pokémon gachapon toys. These include figures and key chains.

Clip 'N' Go

In 2018, Pokémon released the first Clip 'N' Go toys. These toys are Poké Balls containing Pokémon figures. The Poké Balls attach to a Clip 'N' Go belt. More than 100 different Clip 'N' Go toys have been released.

Clip 'N' Go figures come in different types of Poké Balls.

Playsets

Tomy also sells Pokémon playsets. The small sets fit into travel cases. Each travel case unfolds into a setting, such as a mountain or a volcano. Small Pokémon figures and accessories come with each playset. Deluxe playsets include larger settings and movable pieces. These pieces include elevators that move up and down.

There are dozens of Pokémon playsets available.

The first Tamagotchi were released in 1996.

Tamagotchi

Tamagotchi are handheld digital toys. They are made by toy maker Bandai Namco. Tamagotchi are virtual pets. Owners care for their pets to help them grow. Bandai Namco created an Eevee Tamagotchi in 2019.

Plush Toys

Plush toys are among the most popular Pokémon products. Hasbro created the first Pokémon plush toys in 1999. New monsters were added with each game release. Today, there are more than a thousand Pokémon plushies available.

Some Pokémon plush toys are available only in Japan.

Big and Small

Pokémon plush toys come in many sizes. People can buy small plush toy key chains, medium-sized toys, and giant Pokémon plushies large enough to lie on. Some plush toys can be posed. Others are made to sit upright on their own.

Giant Plush Toy

A giant Eevee plush toy was available through a lottery in 2012. A used one later sold for $5,000.

The first Pokémon Squishmallows were released in 2022.

Squishmallows

Squishmallows are plush toys. They are round and extra soft and squishy. Pokémon worked with the company to make Pokémon Squishmallows. More than ten Pokémon Squishmallows have been released. Each costs about $30.

Build-a-Bear

Build-a-Bear is a store that allows people to create their own plushies. Pokémon collaborated with the company to make a line of Build-a-Bear Pokémon. The company sells more than 30 Pokémon plushies. Some of the plushies come with Pokémon-themed clothes.

Build-a-Bear has released plush versions of Squirtle, Vulpix, and Meowth, *left to right*.

My Pikachu

Pikachu is one of Pokémon's most popular creatures. The My Pikachu plush line allows fans to get their own special Pikachu. Each My Pikachu plush toy is a little different. The toys have different sizes, ears, facial expressions, tails, and arm positions. This lets fans have a completely unique toy.

The My Pikachu line launched in 2023.

My Friend Pikachu

My Friend Pikachu is an interactive Pokémon toy. This Pikachu makes more than ten different sounds. When pressed, Pikachu speaks and moves its ears as its cheeks light up.

Monopoly: Pokémon Kanto Edition replaces the game's famous properties with areas in the Kanto region.

Board Games

Pokémon has inspired many board games. These include Pokémon-themed Monopoly and Labyrinth games. There are also original Pokémon board games. Pokémon Master Trainer is a series of board games that mimic the Pokémon video games. Players follow the same journeys as the video games. They roll dice to catch monsters.

FUN FACT!

Several Pokémon-themed editions of Monopoly have been released.

Battle Academy

Pokémon Battle Academy was released in 2020. The game teaches players to play the Pokémon TCG. The pack includes three ready-made card decks. Early versions feature Pikachu, Charizard, and Mewtwo. Newer versions feature Pokémon from later generations.

Each Battle Academy deck contains a rare Full Art card.

MEGA Building Sets

MEGA building sets let fans build their favorite Pokémon. The sets come in pieces. People can build single monsters or entire battle arenas. Some sets include scenes from the Pokémon anime. Evolution sets feature the different evolution stages of Pokémon.

There are more than 60 Pokémon MEGA building sets.

Nanoblocks

Nanoblocks sells sets for creating Pokémon models out of tiny plastic blocks. The sets often have more than 100 pieces. The company also sells sets for building Poké Balls and Pokémon settings. The Mini-Collection creates tiny monsters. Extreme Deluxe models allow people to build Pokémon with posable parts.

Pokémon fans can buy Pokémon shirts, hats, pajamas, and more.

Clothing and Fashion

The Pokémon Center sells lots of themed clothing. Many big stores sell Pokémon-themed shirts and sweaters. Some sell Pokémon-themed socks and shoes. Pokémon designs also appear on suits and dresses. Designer brands such as Tiffany and Fendi have even released Pokémon jewelry and purses.

Costumes

Many people dress as Pokémon characters for Halloween. Some trick-or-treaters dress as trainers. Others dress as Pokémon such as Pikachu or Charizard. People also wear these costumes to Pokémon conventions.

Pokémon costumes come in child and adult sizes.

Arts and Crafts

Pokémon has merchandise for fans who enjoy art. People can buy Pokémon-themed art supplies. These include coloring books and paint-by-number kits. Fans can also buy Pokémon-themed stationery supplies such as notebooks and pens.

Pokémon-themed art supplies are great for fans of all ages.

Visitors to the Van Gogh Museum during its Pokémon collaboration could learn how to draw Pikachu.

Live Art Exhibits

Art fans can attend Pokémon art exhibits. The Van Gogh Museum in the Netherlands worked with Pokémon in 2023 to create an exhibit about the artist Vincent van Gogh. The exhibit included art of Pokémon in Van Gogh's style.

Some drinks at Pokémon Cafés come with Pokémon latte art.

Pokémon Food

Some stores sell Pokémon-themed food. The food is shaped like Pokémon. For example, there are Pokémon-shaped fruit snacks. Japan even has a few Pokémon Cafés. These are restaurants with dedicated Pokémon-themed products.

Home Decor

Pokémon has products for all ages. Adults can buy Pokémon decor for their homes.

The Pokémon Center sells themed waffle makers and dishes. They also sell themed curtains and art. Pokémon is an exciting franchise that all ages can enjoy.

FUN FACT!

Fans can keep up with Pokémon by following the company's official social media accounts.

Pokémon merchandise is available at many major stores.

GLOSSARY

anime
A Japanese cartoon.

convention
An event where people with a shared interest can meet.

crystallized
Made out of crystals.

debut
To make a first appearance.

exclusive
Available only under certain circumstances.

franchise
A brand or business.

game mechanic
A rule or system that controls how a game works.

grader
A professional who rates the quality of collectibles.

illustrator
A person who draws art.

immune
Not affected or harmed.

mainline
Part of the main series of something.

merchandise
Goods that people can buy.

open-world map
A game design that allows players to go anywhere in the world rather than being forced to take a specific route.

region
A part of a larger area.

resistant
Less affected by something.

species
A group of similar creatures.

TO LEARN MORE

More Books to Read

Andreou, Katherine. *Pokémon Book of Evolutions*. DK, 2024.

Pokémon Super Duper Extra Deluxe Essential Handbook. Scholastic, 2024.

Ringstad, Arnold. *The Pokémon Encyclopedia*. Abdo, 2026.

Online Resources

To learn more about Pokémon, please visit **abdobooklinks.com** or scan this QR code. These links are routinely monitored and updated to provide the most current information available.

INDEX

PHOTO CREDITS

Cover Photos: Robert Way/Shutterstock Images, front (Pikachu); Shutterstock Images, front (Squirtle, Eevee, Charmander, Mewtwo); Adobe Stock, front (Pokémon Go); Vladimir Borozenets/Shutterstock Images, back

Interior Photos: Shutterstock Images, 1, 3, 4, 5 (top), 9 (top), 11 (top), 11 (bottom), 12 (top), 12 (bottom), 14 (left), 14 (right), 17, 19 (middle), 21, 22, 23, 28, 29, 44, 54, 56, 58, 59, 60, 61, 64 (top), 67, 68, 69, 70, 72 (top), 72 (bottom), 77 (top), 80, 83 (bottom), 87, 88, 89, 92, 95, 100, 102, 106, 107, 109, 111 (top), 111 (bottom), 118, 121, 124, 125; Kyodo News/Newscom, 5 (bottom); TommL/E+/Getty Images, 6; Jordi Villar/Shutterstock Images, 7; Makoto Miyazaki/Yomiuri Shimbun/AP Images, 8; Maksim Ankuda/Shutterstock Images, 9 (bottom), 64 (bottom); Aksitaykut/Dreamstime, 10, 32, 74; Li Nanxuan/China News Service/Getty Images, 13; Simbert Brause/Shutterstock Images, 15, 55, 63, 65, 66; Christa Kelly/Red Line Editorial, 16, 39, 42, 46, 47, 48, 57, 73, 91, 94, 103, 108, 112, 117, 122; Vladimir Borozenets/Shutterstock Images, 18; Aleksei Egorov/Alamy, 19 (top); Red Line Editorial, 19 (bottom), 25, 82, 84, 86, 96, 99; Shogakukan/Tomy/Kobal/Shutterstock Images, 20; Deviant Art, 24 (top), 31 (types); Acorn 1/Alamy, 24 (bottom); May Tse/South China Morning Post/Getty Images, 26; Hulton Archive/Getty Images, 27; Rajavadivel Hariharan/Shutterstock Images, 30, 33, 34, 35, 36, 37, 40, 49, 50, 101; Zefry Novizar/Shutterstock Images, 31 (Pokémon), 38, 41, 43, 45, 51; Sergei Bachlakov/Shutterstock Images, 52; John Keeble/Getty Images News/Getty Images, 53, 79; Justin Sullivan/Getty Images News/Getty Images, 62; James Manning/PA Images/Getty Images, 71; Warner Bros./AJ Pics/Alamy, 75; Yves Forestier/Sygma/Getty Images, 76; Warner Bros. Pictures/Hulton Archive/Getty Images, 77 (bottom); Andrea Izzotti/Shutterstock Images, 78; John Hanson Pye/Shutterstock Images, 81; Russell Savage/Dreamstime, 83 (top); iStockphoto, 85, 90, 93; Sadie Mantell/Shutterstock Images, 97, 98; Stefan Lambauer/Shutterstock Images, 104; El Fithni/Shutterstock Images, 105; Zhang Xiaoyu/Xinhua News Agency/Getty Images, 110; Patti McConville/Alamy, 113; Henry Saint John/Shutterstock Images, 114; Piranhi/Alamy, 115; Courtesy of The Strong National Museum of Play, Rochester, New York, USA, 116; Wachiwit/Dreamstime, 119; Jean-Claude Deutsch/Paris Match Archive/Getty Images, 120; ANP/Alamy, 123